VALC

Hamn

C000055842

ISBN: 978-1-913642-42-6

Book designed by Aaron Kent

Edited by Aaron Kent

Broken Sleep Books (2021), Talgarreg, Wales

Contents

Desperation
Fog   9
'Outside, the twerpy birds flit mad'   10
Is this the Real Life   11
Folk poem   13
'Finnish was the language I was going to learn'   14
Walden   16
Fred West's Cardigan   18

Pacification
Blue   23
Hirim, Hirim and on   24
Deer   25
The Wait   27
Magpie   28
'A child's fingertips'   29
September   31

Expectation
'Grief has the same secrecy'   35
Evelyn   36
The Wait   37
'You have never met such a wizard'   38
Wrong poem   39
Me^2 40
'Untangling myself from the sheets and rolling'   41

Acclamation
Holiday   45
Not just grief but Marks & Sparks   46
Charlotte   47
'Halloween comes at the best time,'   48
Mark flies home to Baby   49
Iron Like a Lion   50
'Black forest,'   51

Realisation

Mother's Day   55
Poem for a Sprite   56
'Cluster lilies in their blue fire thrust'   57
for Aldous   58
Spring is the King   59
'If it were up to me you'd be'   60
'It starts in the toes'   61

Acknowledgements   63

Valour

Emma Hammond

And the world opened out. And a day was good to awaken to. And there were no limits to anything. And the people of the world were good and handsome. And I was not afraid anymore.

– **John Steinbeck**

Desperation

Fog

There is a decent amount of stillness
in snow, and also in the yellow of daffodils.
It would be easy to say they remind me of you,
but they don't. The crown of each
burns. All around, people

are effortlessly people, some elsewhere.
Poets are ghosts. It is not especially
romantic. Stillness and the urge to participate,
hoping the snow sits- casting out lines, always
wonky, the agony! Sounds good does it.

Yet right at the crux, bright amber. Suspended,
knowing our faces are lunatic gaps in some
bottomless armour. So far into absurd that
cash is unfathomable, hearts birthing
bright from our sleeves like hernia. Still,

the need to be a part of it, to have existed-
to never forget that we are slipping away
all miracle. Vivid and extra, skin and light,
experiments in weather. To touch, to write it
right. Staying open in the only way we

Outside, the twerpy birds flit mad
special into the sunlight. The dog's ears
robo-swivel to the drama of rustling ivy,
unravelling like an unwound cassette.

Fox-bothered pots, imperial in carnelian
drape themselves over shingle,
business-like over the brown shouting
of spilled soil. Dog finds a hurt yellow

balloon, popped dead on the forecourt
and tries to kill himself. Items revolve
through his sharky mouth, impish sticks
and pink bits of flip flops- he chews on

the cryptic roots in unending query.
Far away, the sound of a seabird sends
him quivery, whiskers all hi in electric-
rigid as clockwork and strange as a loop.

Is this the Real Life

Yearning for the sea,
something about a white boarded pod
and down the road a smokehouse
that wraps the fish in silence, dog.
If I were asked I might say it was hot

white horses, some crashing. A trip out
each day to the sweet shop to see Graveling
with the big old ears like bacon, how
do we get there. TV in the evenings
and a simple meal of Gothel, Coke float.

Downed with light brown hair, despair-
it was your voice on the line, you unmet me.
Prying open my day like a mouth, you
muddied my pearl. I am not interested
in you and your lack of poetry,

don't care for your aggregate view,
trying to squeeze your body into the hours
like a fat old foot, rushing for trains, moral
mathematics then skating on the surface
like some finely shanked bug.

I am not interested in hurting or filling your
silences with reupped words- I research
the most awful things. The sun opens a
cloud like a curious knife, the grass is
a various city, I don't have time, I'm

aiming for the shore. The crunk of shingle
and the roseate cubes that shrink you,
targeted toward the gaggle of girls that
carve up sand and play in ribbons-
unwatched, there's no display.

The games of the ardent bore me.
While on the tide we flutter- roaming
in wellies, in ourselves, out. Lost
to the deep we strain to conch
the loud black aches of a mermaid.

Folk poem

1.

Clean me

2.

Also available in white

3.

I wish my wife was as dirty as this

Finnish was the language I was going to learn from Linguaphone. It was glamorous and also my cat Sid was from Finland, he had his stuffing knocked out when the maggots got in him and we had to put him in the washing machine. I needed to discuss it with him, and also how the boys had got him in the playground one day and threw him around until I cried a bit but was brave and didn't show it.

I was going to learn Finnish, so I saved my money and one day went to the post box opposite my school so I could post the Important Forms off and get the tapes which I would listen to on my Walkman. Then I would be able to talk with Sid, about all the things, and he would listen to the things and that would be OK.

The post box was all on it's own on a V shaped verge and over the road was my school where somewhere behind a fence was a shed with a secret music box where a small plastic woman went round and round. Also there was a whole hedge full of ghosts, but I was the only one who knew and the daddy long legs skipped around them with this big silence, I never knew what it was but I did know about death.

I was in trouble. I was always in trouble. I was in trouble because I didn't know how to tie my shoelaces or tell the time. No one ever told me how to do those things and I thought I was pretty dumb. Sid came everywhere, he was stretchy and his eyes were scratched from where the boys had got him, also a dog had once bitten his ears a bit so he was all ragged but I made him clothes that were glamorous like his *Arabian Nights* costume and he wore a jam pot frill as a hat and sang songs about being a pop star.

I was a witch but no one knew, and there was a witch above my head but also out in the orchard and no one knew about that one except the bats. Maybe I would tell Sid once I was fluent in Finnish, I think he would be interested and that would be pretty good. There were lots of things I wanted to talk about and although I was *obtuse* I'm pretty sure that he wouldn't mind because he was not brand new.

All the things in Beauty and the Beast came alive, there was a candlestick that could talk and also a clock, I think he was French. I'm sure that the post box was alive too- he was red and his mouth was open but nothing ever came out and he didn't seem as friendly as the little teacup with the chip. In fact if you put your hand in there with Important Forms then it was very possible your hand would get bitten off which would make tying your shoes up even more difficult.

One day they burned the fields around him, and the black smoke rose up and swallowed him and the ghosts and the little lady all to nothing. I stole a handkerchief off a girl and buried it in the woods. I would have kept it but it had her initials on in curly stitch and in the end it didn't have much to do with me.

Walden

Night-clothed
over-seer
manna-wise
wood-chuck

Noon-day
elm-tree
hill-top
toad-stools

Wood-side
saddle-bow
home-made
bean-field

Low-lived
door-sill
in-dweller
beggar-ticks

Huckle-berry
pickerel-weed
piece-meal
butter-flies

Sap-wood
drill-barrow
john's-wort
fir-trees

Golden-rod
tip-toe
wood-chopper's
scare-crow

Half-witted
empty-handed
no-one
Ech-o

Fred West's Cardigan

written at Ledbury

The sun so vicious hot the tarmac burnt
the Spanish intern's instep mid Flamenco,
Fred. I searched for the long gone Youth Club-
right forgotten at the poetry festival, run

by this African Rifles vet called Ken. You probably
knew of him within the jungle din of rumbling bikes,
your gypsy looks and grin, the bramble hair, all that.
The girl that smacked you up the escape

on Bye Street to the Homend where kids
still skulk in stilts, too bored to grope and eating
hands by stalls of drizzle. Scrim, more bloody
melting tea under a scowl of weightless breasts.

The Milk Bar's ghost where you met Rena,
lassoed with dirty promise, a cavernous mouth
of bragging entire wildness, a sausage plait
of shame the poets hanker on. Refined; Can the

air be more rarefied do you think? Do you miss
the knife-sharp bunting? Would I put on your cardigan
in this godforsaken heat, the woollen embrace of a
scrambled animal, pre-Rose, like rape- some home?

Pacification

Blue

Across a reddening ocean
of tangled cables, sinew,
or by a white bloody van upon
a bridge that does not reach,

one by every one the kids
get pulled like toyless crackers.
Old moons, familiar soils. still,
the crones warn us in bullets

love is abstract, childish.
We suffer their unreal flag
in swathes of crime tape-
hyperbole, traditions of sickness,

a terrible romance, these apes.

Hirim, Hirim and on

Some of those beetles are so shiny
they look like tiny bits of glass
before the tide whipped them
about in a washing machine

The honeysuckle is in tip-top condition,
the smell is arguably better
than freshly cut grass,
which everyone is always a fan of

There is a black thing in the tree,
it is possibly an amputated leg
cut neat through the middle,
tied around with string to keep the sock up

Out of the window a cat
watches with burning eyes
as the bells of an ice-cream van
shatter the air into a thousand wafers

Deer

"I used Helen Mort's poem as a model for my own but rushed and ended up submitting a draft that wasn't entirely my own work" - Christian Ward

I stepped up
towards mother pines
on the brighter moor,

I saw where five deer
more ragged than
the rose that flickered
lapped every God
to water,

I followed the river back
like each of the otters
at Ullapool did
for them and who/
whatever waited I
at the garden's edge.

The night that never
followed stood on
through fur supple eyes
they-darned in mother,

and Rannoch forest
graceful from
the kingfisher south
where we saw the night
stealing in-between
time,

the pound-coin holidays
she brought out to hers,
the watched ones
looking for their ribs,
and those swears that saw them
the same before teatime.

I must have been
that window in my middle
because I have
no memory of them,
of the house we were then-
the years more
coloured than the trees,
fish-bone closer
than hooves.

The Wait

The old ship left, creaking into the chop & good-
bye to you. Another month with empty arms &
the racket of other people's luck, tiny little eyelids,
the slight smell of burning from a fontanelle.

Off you go. I am waiting for ze blood to come, it is
baptism, a renewal of hope. They say relax it'll be
your big opening soon, I say forget it. Ego's overrated,
the whole point is to give & it seems I cannot do that.

Sandy tears for the tiny speck of morse-flecked
light that circles my Shangri-la, wanting a go. It is
missing me, wants a grow of skin to slip into,
for me to give it a bit of a stroke- old Niblet.

Honestly, perhaps I am not destined to love that hard-
it is hard. More to give the oak-eyed olds a break
& call those quickstep children as my own. OK then!
We are all one after all. A writhing mass of golden fleece.

Magpie

One for joy
Two for joy
Three for joy
Four for joy
Five for joy
Six for joy
Seven for joy
Eight for joy
Nine for joy
Ten for joy

1.

A child's

fingertips like 10 distant stars
reach toward me,
lost
in perhaps. My inability

to use a sextant,
scrabbling round
to land you
on my H

to the sound of a choir
of freckles. I will lie
to you. How close I am
to earth! Virtually
underground,
a white horse
chalked in blood.

Have I failed to bring you
out of myself?
If I could love you
alone into me, I would.

I search the house
to dig you out
with astrolabe,
to tend you right
through fiery hoops
as rain.

2.

Rolodex of stars,
you have probably
already died
a thousand times over,
the light I see is only just
travelled here.

I wait in my plastic chair,
and write quiet essays
on Bushido,
stuck in lists-

my two cold hands
like swans of ice.

September

Waking in September is
half great half death-
the sexy low sun that pierces
your eyes and the wailing

Of the washing machine. O
sadness, the softener is all
gone, the trees are killing
themselves all over the place-

You are wedged in your bed
like a loose tooth. The imminent
bare-sole pain of the coldy tiles-
the depression! Smudges on

The wall, your mouth, the alarm-
a bastard. White skies undress
in the tsk tsk of autumn rain,
and the summer cries *evil*! Dead.

Expectation

Grief has the same secrecy
as an empty tic-tac box filled with
puddle water. The parachuting
man we hid in the petrol cap
of your Mum's car, quick stolen-
the handkerchief I buried in the trees.

I liked the embroidery. I like it now,
this grief and its stitches, it makes
me flower even through snot. Things
fly past the planet, roaring. I like
the axis, the counting down. Nostalgia
a cutie, bean-filled Totoro.

The whirl of fur he lived in; His ancient
teeth that ripped me, the bad quality.
We went all over the world in love.
Paws are unshook hands- yet I'm shaken.
Don't worry dog, I'll find you. In galaxies,
through death. I'll always be your person.

Evelyn
poem for a niece

This early bird, her face
crumpled and cheek
struck, wisps,

a tiny pip, red like dawn-
spilled fields the same
way rose-gold rolls up

from the tongue.
Autumn one, scrumpling
moon-bright as an apple

from a well lit grove,
lips soft-fixed in *Hello world,
so this is today then!*

Her name in flowers, Evelyn.

Jr

Supposing there is a tiny kernel of life
lodged somewhere behind the furious wave
of your ailing masculinity, know this-

we are not for you. We are not for your
tears as the shock of cold air hits you
square in the gullet. More stoic

than you understand, we wait, can see
the desperate boy, red as an egg,
your failed excuse. Buoyed with need,

the *big man*- hear your foghorn, feel
the scrabbling, all the -ests then more,
most right, most loud, most sexed.

And all behind your blinds of meat,
the old days gripe- that time you touched
the sleeping girl, the feels you copped,

the castles built and smashed. You know
we know, your default fear, some idiot pride,
your fingers dank with beer, with blood,

the well paid plans that never birth. Don't
sweat it kid, you're still alive but brinked
inept, some weaker sex- unclothed.

You have never met such a wizard
as this wizard. He is an extreme wizard
with the markings of a blood-dipped finger
placed firm across his outer cheek.

He keeps onward threading his specialty
bolts hard across her menacing sky, offers
Lichtenberg knotweed, bright coral, roots.
She accepts the wild creeping snakes

of burning matter partly in her dreadful
mouth; They hiss and pop in the cold n
olden cavern of her. At some point he is
planning to kill her in half and turn her to glass,

to hurtle right through her like light.

Wrong poem

It is tipping on its rockers
and slops to the edge of the bucket, its runners.

The girl is propelled to the floor she's been knitting,
and the rocker sits back on two smiles.

Me²

Leaves chuck themselves onto tracks, flashers
in their airy clearings. A stack of mags called Hot
Chicks, the haunted caravan in Weeley, Essex,
haunted with Essex. My roving 12 year old mind

like a priest in a lady of wicker- a rubbish witch,
dropped off at dawn to the seafront toilets where the
mirrors are sheets of metal. Dark tearooms of fudge
and lingering death. The fracas of rain on a skylight

which cuts. Wore his t-shirt in bed for months,
breasts pressed flat in penance, the neck too
high, the way he called his sister *slag*. Girls burn
the lanes, as fiery dollies of corn that flicker

bright then slip down cracks to London. Holed up
in hedgerows with glo-worms and peat, mocking
the plimsoll line scribbled within; Keeping our openings
close and slight, a watchful glassy silence ftw

Untangling myself from the sheets and rolling
around I see your smile and it's vast as a moon,
your spider hand comes down onto my face
which is a face lined with worry and black
marks round the eyes and crust.

Hello you say. Hello to you, waking up and
considering tea and all the things, like cash
flow and how to change the world by inventing
a robot super race that is not human in the
best ways. Hello softness. Your mouth is the

exact warmth of Spring, but also wet and dark
like soil. Your eyes are mostly full of laughing and
I am pretty sure it is at me. I think this is absolutely
right and my crow's feet crinkle up into a million
different roads to take and this is also very good.

I expect we shall be King and Queen.

Acclamation

Holiday

Clean shelter and bounding dogs between the lake
and I for miles. A queen in the fresh mountain air,
up above furrows and vines arranged in perfect
portions, a full-fat exercise book of juicy maths.

Not a mountain person with this pouch, a little twinge
in the back of the knees, cold-stuck in coffee, art,
watching, don't care if you're better than me, it's nice
here. The air is elevated and sends me dreams of

dead babies, a party at which I am weightless, pig
ballerina. I rot in the pool like a lily pad, dangerous
underwater as a sister. The unicorn has popped,
grappled in fabulous rodeo, the horn gone down.

Not my Dad. I am on holiday and keep working
to fill up the silence. We hear a story about a
bricklayer whose fingers stuck fast in a pulley,
crow hard at absurdity, dress light.

Not just grief but Marks & Sparks

tights what leave a mouth around your waist.
She probably opens in different ways, a small
aperture; A large glass of wine half a bottle.

If you snap open your peepers through the murk and static
somewhere there on the bloody horizon lies *Securitas*.

It is a sinking city and the inhabitants grow lacy webs
like doilies between their toes. The walls are cakes-
it is a place of pain.

We am bound to get fused
like the chin and neck in an acid attack- to be one
like a single crow on a lorry, bled together like sense,
your duty a dull grey throb that pulses nil.

Outside are stretches of tears, cat hair, long days
of pouting at Mr Death like a milkless christ. Men

to battle on Relevant Subjects, the endless teachings
of older women, wrapped in disappointment like
mystical roadside hags.

You travel back in and grapple with an artifact.
It is a rolling pin, yet the end is covered in human tissue.

You recall your mother reversing into a motorcyclist.
I could have fucking killed him

that queer sort of joy,
quickening her hips into life

Charlotte

poem for a gosh-daughter

Bean-toed
wonder of the Copt
and tiniest
marsh-ling,
bright eyed
supergirl
tied
in bluebells
& sea-lavender-
pink as a
an Essex sky.

Halloween comes at the best time,
a drip down your heart in a churn
of words called oof- this ghost-lit
bad brain hook on one withered hand it

scratches itself in a forest etc, Christ
it's racy. Quick- resurface the jingling spit
says headless / sleepless- nobody
likes you. Thanks ghoul! Do keep me

posted I say, it is helpful to know where
I'm not. Fake blood in the whisper chain,
the dithering rain- childless strings of
lights in tooth, static, pickaxe, how

do you do. Deconstructed in laser sharp
glee- my ribcage a synth, fanning out hard
into the red of black trees. The umami runs
deep. Pls help. I am above, I am nowhere.

Mark flies home to Baby

for Mark E. Smith

You were on my cassette up in my ears with your
violence. My walkman was a scratchy portal straight
to your gammy mouth. I liked it, and the tight sound
of the drums, mounted with the skin of pigeons.

I was also frightened but not of anything.
The time the kids spat on my woollen shelf and
stoic as a pink sparkler, I knew you knew. In your
tank top, casting flames from your ancient hanky.

Something dumb and vicious that ran through all of it.
The ditches laced with porn, distaste in the kitchen-
I knew it. In our world apart, the southern quarters,
we knew the flailing, social hurt. I hid in woodlands

and heard the silence, we were better after all. You
in the gnarled old roots, a latchkey in the darkening
cover and I, proper with my bronze spoon, my
residuals, my uncanny face all flattened by

witches and tarmac. Now gone, into the farflung
corners of the disco. Cosmic gargoyle, rings
of smoke around your ankles like A-OK, and
up in your thorax, the flickering burden of joy.

Iron like a Lion

A mountain, I think. You are one and your dark clouds
brown-uncurl big fat rain on me. You are multi-amazing
like a monument of *molten orange spraying tigers* that spell
you.

Zealous with a cigar that gift-wraps my face in smoky grot,
that bit there is red in my eye and stings, I am still in case
it rolls cold upon my neck-

you're *there* and you tell me in your puff
pastry words about escape and the future,
precision.

I get it I think. I thought about it before
when I saw you rise from the bath
like from Scooby-Doo, penis

waving and your hairy strange enormous brain,
the drip drip drip of a tap,

and concluded that really I am
the woman is, not man does-
a wisp what drifts.

You are my non-killing smooth handed automaton.
I open mine and see maps. My hands are welted
and if you follow this line,

you'll see it leads all the way to Jerusalem.

Black forest,
your hair is
full of thieves and
murderers.

Chop off my head
and bang it
on the roof of
my car.

Like a monkey in
the monkey part,
rip out my aerial.
Lick my hand, why not

give it a whirl, Kirschwasser!

I am a member of
Schwarzwaldverein
and will regulate you up-

sleep in your gorge
of cuckoos.

Realisation

Mother's Day

We have elders that are made of ash,
they try their best, they die, you came
like blood, gentle as a clay hut. You
grow up quick, the gods say no, say

off you go. We sail to boys, the soil,
the kids go round and soon they know
how short we come, how narrow- though
you must not ever think I do not love you.

Poem for a Sprite

Oh Hai canary, I see you
climb. If I were a mine then
you would come up singing
radical, a silver-edged

fresh yellow pipe with white
sound, pine moondial. & how
bird- magicked, our best trick,
are you glued only by light?

The years of feeding Twiglets
through neverending channels of
canvas, trying to make a home of
me, for you eggling. Now you spur

with courage, the burgeoning heat
of a bobbin. Don't fret birdie,
we'll spin our endless nest from
every better thing we ever did

and you can rest, quiet in your
pink terrarium. So, buffering in
your life pod, we'll do for you,
and you will do for everything.

Cluster lilies in their blue fire thrust
up through Wednesday morning.
Tomorrow will be the same like those

falling Dominoes that go up and over
and around, or mattresses too,
all people going backwards on YouTube.

They are like that. I like it, the simplicity,
these flowers will brown and I will buy some
more, doodle them onto the vase

with an immediate pencil. Days go by
in some kind of sequence but suddenly
I am old. When I dream of Goblin Hill

and I am always 12- a tooth we
dissolved in Coke, I think: In 100 years
we will all be dead. It's as hard to imagine

as space- or the softness of Mum's
upper arms. They existed and Honey &
Betsy too. Such tenderness in every

rickety synapse, built-in, see-through.
All we ever can say is I love you brave wraith-
I will always forever love you.

for Aldous

In the pink room we have found
each other- you in the blue sling
and I deep in the dreams that
I have for you. It is raining post
heatwave and I am glad your tiny
feet are cold as shells, my heart-
beat pressed up hard against
your ear. Nothing can touch us

now. Your duckling hair is real
as you are, I never thought we'd
get this far. I had you in mind for
so long you're still made up, an
unbuilt world. Sometimes you
chirp and I realise you're here,
hot little hands in a grip, how
serious you are. When your eyes

open they are in flint, intent,
certain in some cold burning that
you've been here before. Wrap me
up in that, I like it. I like you a lot
small policeman. You are the icing
on the ocean- a dot! And when you're
asleep I transcribe every breath,
golden crest, tiny bird, new entire.

Spring is the King

Spring is delicious in flames and ginger,
the dead dog's tree is opening out right-
buds with the smallest flickering of
acid house in the tip, finally and all after
we had given it up. In a green grotto
of tangled birdsong, the gloveless axis

smashes it up into April. Pan says
we are not allowed outside, it suits me fine,
for only the forest is sad without the old gang,
me and doggin. I had not been up there,
for to clock the loss of together would be
too much, right. Kinga was vivid, every old lady

would fizz and cry such a beautiful dog. And he was.
a scrap of cosmos in the trees, his white trousers
at the back bobbing along under his hackle-white
tail- everyone loved that god. This year we are
not allowed outside, but it suits me down to
the ground- old world with its all kinds of glitches,

some good stuff like cinema and magicians,
but mostly ice. They've gone and done it now,
the whole of the everything's shut. The place in
Sprinkletti but it's not so bad, just an egg-coloured
ghost with dark wailings of Easter all in scrambles-
I'm opted out, see. Spring is the king and I'm free.

1.

If it were up to me you'd be
made of cable

in artisan socks from
Iceland, Eigg or Hoth.

Even in June, in June
I want to keep you

bundled, call you toast
and soft and close as

microwaved milk
in a crumpet oubliette.

2.

Ready Brek jet setter,
your crown a fiery hob,

Top of the Pops and bonfire
fudge, nestled in fleece

honey, middle encased
in a crucible of cashmere-

forever sleep cosy in tog 3.5
my tiny love, fisherman's friend.

It starts in the toes
of a ropey morning,
the passing of summer,
the open-eyed pastures,
a lounging in stasis,
done. Your toes,

and they say useless, say
done. And they say how well
you alienated the lot of it-
pals. The scene... you did it!
Became one

with the absolute inward,
silent hour- it carries you,
alone as a craft. Bears

weight, the days like
puffs that end in an echo,
as Sugar Puffs or
clouds with their silver
slices, your snacks,
your snacks, some
frisson of sadness, O
toes-

what will you do once the
Autumn descends upon leaves
upon the leaves? They
hang on your every

Acknowledgements

For my favourites- Dan, Flo and Indy
& to Kingsley, the best of all good boys x

LAY OUT YOUR UNREST